abundant life

An 8-Week Bible Study for Groups or Individuals

rebekah freed

Copyright © 2024 Rebekah Freed

All rights reserved. No part of this publication may be reproduced, distributed, or transmitted in any form or by any means, without prior written permission of the author, except in the case of brief quotations embodied in critical reviews and certain other noncommercial uses permitted by copyright law.

Unless otherwise indicated, all Scripture quotations are from The ESV® Bible (The Holy Bible, English Standard Version®), © 2001 by Crossway, a publishing ministry of Good News Publishers. Used by permission. All rights reserved.

Scripture quotations marked (NLT) are taken from the Holy Bible, New Living Translation, copyright ©1996, 2004, 2015 by Tyndale House Foundation. Used by permission of Tyndale House Publishers, Carol Stream, Illinois 60188. All rights reserved.

Scripture quotations marked (NIV) are taken from the Holy Bible, New International Version®, NIV®. Copyright © 1973, 1978, 1984, 2011 by Biblica, Inc.™ Used by permission of Zondervan. All rights reserved worldwide. www.zondervan.comThe "NIV" and "New International Version" are trademarks registered in the United States Patent and Trademark Office by Biblica, Inc.™

To the students of
Concordia University, Nebraska
May you always be filled with
the abundant life and love of Jesus

study overview

Week 1	A God of Life	Pg. 7
Week 2	Life Begins	Pg. 19
Week 3	Life Shattered	Pg. 29
Week 4	A Resurrected Life	Pg. 39
Week 5	Living with Hope	Pg. 49
Week 6	A Life of Purpose	Pg. 59
Week 7	Living in Freedom	Pg. 71
Week 8	Life Forever	Pg. 81

Jesus said, "The thief comes only to steal, kill, and destroy. I came that they may have life and have it abundantly."
John 10:10

As We Begin

I am so grateful you have joined me on this journey. While this is designed as an eight-week study, there is nothing that says you have to make sure to get through this in a certain number of days. The most important part of any study is simply connecting with God through His Word. Give yourself grace and avoid shame or guilt if you miss a day or two. Just pick it back up and keep moving forward. This, too, is a way to practice abundant life in Jesus, a life of freedom and grace.

This study was created with the hope that it could be used for group or individual study. The structure has one long session for each week followed by five readings to dig deeper into God's Word.

STUDYING WITH OTHERS

Studying God's Word is often richer and more fun with other people. So, find a friend (or ten) and go through the study together! I would encourage you to begin your study each week in prayer, asking God to guide your time together and open your eyes to what He wants to show you.

The questions provided throughout the weekly study sessions can be used with the entire group or in smaller groups or pairs. Each session ends with some questions that would be ideal to process in groups of around three people. You can also use that small group time to share prayer requests and pray for each other.

INDIVIDUAL STUDY

If using this as a personal study, you can reflect personally on the questions provided. I also encourage you to consider starting a conversation with a friend about one or more of the questions each week. Hearing from others about these topics enhances our own understanding of abundant life. Part of truly living is remembering we are not alone. For the longer weekly sessions, feel free to break the questions up over a few days as needed.

Here we go! Let's LIVE!

week 1

A God of Life

One day a while back I found myself sitting in a chapel service at the college where I work, discouraged at all the pain, hurt, and despair I saw our students experiencing day after day. My teammate Ryan, the campus pastor, got up to pray. In addition to our normal prayers for those who were sick or grieving and situations going on in the world, he also prayed for the department where I work, the Student *Life* Office. Something about the way in which he emphasized the word "life" stuck with me long after we walked out of chapel that day. I couldn't get it out of my head. As the next few days unfolded, God brought **John 10:10** to my mind over and over. Here Jesus says:

"The thief comes only to steal, kill, and destroy. I came that they may have life and have it abundantly."

That verse captured so much of what I was experiencing and seeing in the world around me in that season. Students and teammates at the college were constantly stressed and overwhelmed with all the expectations piling up. Multiple friends were walking through some of the most devastating moments in their marriages and families. A student had died a few weeks before and the impact of that trauma was wide-reaching. Yet, over the months following that moment, I found myself eager to explore the concept of life—full, rich, satisfying life. Despite the ways I saw Satan stealing, killing, and destroying in that season, I came to experience this truth as well: Jesus brings life.

Where do you see Satan stealing, killing, and destroying in your life, the lives of your friends and family, or in the communities around you?

When those kinds of challenges or disappointments are present in our lives, it is easy to go into survival mode. We may find it challenging to consider what it looks like to "thrive" when we can barely make it through the day.

So, what *does* abundant life look like?

Here are some things that come to mind for me:
- It looks like a contented smile at the end of a purpose-filled day.
- It sounds like little kids giggling with delight.
- It is having margin in our schedule to joyfully care for a need that arises for someone we love or even a stranger.
- It is a community that talks honestly about hard things and doesn't make us feel like we must put on a mask.
- It's belonging and believing we have a purpose in this world.
- It feels like we can breathe again.

Now it's your turn! What could abundant life look like for you? What does it sound like or maybe even taste like? It may take a little imagination, especially if you feel like you're in a season of survival, but take some time to dream a little. What might it feel like to be fully alive? (*If you are studying with a group talk about this in pairs and then share with the larger group.*)

Story after story and verse after verse in scripture point to the fact that our God is a God of LIFE! **Look up the verses in the following chart and write the names or descriptions of God next to the Bible reference.**

NAME OF GOD	BIBLICAL REFERENCE
	John 11:25
	Luke 20:38
	1 John 1:1
	John 6:35
	John 14:6
	Jeremiah 10:10
	1 Peter 2:4
	2 Corinthians 3:3
	Acts 3:15

Here are a few more names and descriptions for God:
- Our Life - Colossians 3:4
- Living Water - John 4
- The Living Father - John 6:57
- Prince of Life - Acts 3:15
- Son of the Living God - Matthew 16:16
- The Living One - Revelation 1:18
- The Spirit of Life - Romans 8:2
- Him Who Lives Forever - Revelation 10:6
- Shepherd of My Life - Genesis 48:15

Depending on which English translation you use, there are up to twenty-four names for God that all include the word "life" or "living." This tells us something about His character and focus.

Throughout the next eight weeks, we're going to dig into stories throughout the Bible, from Genesis to Revelation, that will prayerfully:
- Reveal more about this Living God,
- Open our eyes to the spaces in our lives He longs to bring life and resurrection, and
- Show us how to practically live this abundant life and invite others into life as well.

John, one of Jesus' disciples, wrote the book of the Bible that bears that same name. He saw what Jesus did. He followed Him. He loved Him not just as a teacher and God but also as a friend. The stories he could have written about Jesus were countless, but he had to select just a few to include. Near the end of the book that he wrote to document Jesus' life, he wrote these words:

> *"Jesus performed many other signs in the presence of his disciples, which are not recorded in this book. But these are written that you may believe that Jesus is the Messiah, the Son of God,* **and that by believing you may have life in his name***"*
> *(John 20:30-31, NIV - emphasis added).*

John seemed to pick up on this theme as well:
Our God is a God of life.

John specifically chose the stories he included in his Gospel—many of which we'll get to explore together throughout the weeks ahead—so that we would find LIFE in Jesus!

As this first week of study comes to a close, consider where God might want to restore life in the next eight weeks.

**What is an area in your life that feels a little dead?
Who is God bringing to mind that needs a resurrection story?
Where is Satan stealing, killing, or destroying and
you long for Jesus to break in and bring life?**

You are invited to write whatever comes to mind in the space on the next page titled "Praying for Life". You can come back to that page again and again, as often as you remember in the next eight weeks, to pray and speak life over these situations, struggles, or people.

When finished, continue with the small group or personal reflection questions on page 12.

praying for life

Jesus, bring life! Amen!
Let's watch in hopeful expectation of what He might do!

Small Group Discussion or Personal Reflection:

What are you most looking forward to about this Abundant Life study and what do you hope to get out of it?

As you consider the names of God on page 9, is there one that captured your attention? What about it seems meaningful to you in this moment?

At whatever level of detail you are comfortable with, share with a friend or your small group something about what you wrote on your "Praying for Life" page. Where are you asking God for new life or resurrection right now?

Talk through the "Digging Deeper" invitation on pages 13-14, share any prayer requests, and close in prayer.

digging deeper
An Invitation

One way Jesus often brings life is through the life-giving rhythms of prayer and regularly reading His Word, the Bible.

Each week of the study you'll have a chance to dig deeper into the themes and scriptures on your own. This practice is meant to be full of grace and LIFE, not duty, obligation, or shame.

If reading God's Word on your own is a new practice for you or if you are in a particularly busy season of life, consider starting with just five minutes a day. Others of you may be able to spend significant amount of time exploring these scriptures, reflecting, and in prayer. The most important part is simply showing up to this time with Jesus and asking Him to use it to bring life.

If you miss a day, don't stress out about it. Just pick up with the next one and enjoy that time with Jesus in His Word.

Each week has a similar rhythm to follow for suggested readings and reflections. Some of the readings will continue looking into the themes we studied in that week's lesson while others will look ahead to next week's study. You can use the pages provided or your own journal to note your reflections each day.

At the bottom of each weekly "Digging Deeper" page, there is a spot for you to write other prayer requests for the week. If you are doing this study with a group, you can write the prayer requests of your group members there. Enjoy your time with Jesus this week!

week 1
Digging Deeper

read
Read today's passage from the Bible:
Day 1 - Colossians 3:1-11
Day 2 - Psalm 16
Day 3 - Genesis 2:4-25
Day 4 - John 1:1-8
Day 5 - Romans 8:1-11

write
Pick one or two verses from today's reading and write it out on the next few reflection pages provided or in your journal.

reflect
Use one or all of the following questions to reflect on the verses you read today:
1. Why did I pick the verse I did to write out? Are there any specific words or phrases that stood out to me?
2. What does today's reading tell me about God/Jesus?
3. What does today's reading tell me about abundant life?
4. What does this reading lead me to pray or do today?

prayer requests for this week:

week 1 notes & reflections

week 2
Life Begins

Think back to the events of your life this week, last week's study, or your time alone with Jesus in His Word. What is something you learned or re-learned about God this past week OR what is a question that came up as you studied?

Today we are going to start at the very beginning—the beginning of our story as human beings. The beginning of the world itself. We find the story of the beginning of life in the very first book of the Bible, Genesis. The first chapter outlines God speaking into existence light, stars, plants, animals, and more. Near the end, God has one more important creation...US!
Let's read about it in Genesis 1:26-31.
What do you learn about life from these verses?

As we continue into Genesis chapter 2, the author begins re-telling some of what happened in chapter 1, this time in greater detail. Throughout chapter 1, we read about all that God spoke into existence. As we get ready to read the more detailed version of God creating humans in chapter 2, note how He did it.
Read Genesis 2:5-25.
What do these verses tell us about God as a God of life?

Humans were *formed* from the dust of the ground and God *breathed* life into man. Everything else He just spoke into creation; humans He touched and breathed into. From the very beginning, God has been in relationship with humans. Touch and breath involve nearness. He didn't just yell across the cosmos with us; He was actively and intimately involved—digging in the dirt, breathing life.

He not only gave humans life and breath, He sustains our life to this day. **Job 33:4** says,
> *"The Spirit of God has made me,*
> *and the breath of the Almighty gives me life."*

Isaiah 42:5-7 tells us more about God as the Creator and Sustainer of life as well as our purpose:
> *"Thus says God, the LORD, who created the heavens and stretched them out, who spread out the earth and what comes from it,* **who gives breath to the people on it and spirit to those who walk in it:** *'I am the LORD; I have called you in righteousness; I will take you by the hand and keep you; I will give you as a covenant for the people, a light for the nations, to open the eyes that are blind, to bring out the prisoners from the dungeon, from the prison those who sit in darkness'"* (emphasis added).

God brings life and breath.

This echoes what we learned back in the first session in John 10:10 — Jesus came to bring life. And He does it so we can bring life as well. Part of living the abundant life God has for us is inviting others into that abundance.

Circling back to Genesis, let's look at a few other details.
First, which tree(s) is/are in the middle of the garden?

Tuck that information away for future weeks.
The language in chapter 2 about trees and rivers echoes some other passages. **Read Jeremiah 17:7-8.** This shows a picture of living an abundant life. So does **John 15:1-9.**
As you read those scriptures, consider: What helps us abide? What helps us stay rooted near the water? What helps us stay connected to the source of life?

Now, let's think back to what we already read in **Genesis 1 and 2**. What do we learn about living and God's original design for life from this small section of scripture that happened before sin and brokenness appeared?

In this story we see five Ps that describe what life was like. Some of these you may have already discovered on your own, maybe just in different words. As you read each one, consider where in the passage you see that concept at play (e.g. God *provided* food and companionship).

Perfection - We can't comprehend complete perfection, but it was present in the garden. A truly perfect life.

Provision - He provided for them in abundance everything they could need, including each other.

Protection - He protected them through the boundaries He gave, as well as His presence.

Purpose - They had work to do, a call to be fruitful and oversee aspects of God's beautiful creation. They had a purpose in the world. This is part of an abundant life.

Personal Relationship with God – They had an intimate, personal, conversational, day-to-day relationship with the God of the Universe. We will see more of this when we look at Genesis 3.

It's important to consider God's original intent for life as we attempt to truly *live* instead of just survive or exist. You might have heard these popular sayings about life:
"Life is unfair. You get what you get."
"Life's short and then you die."

That's not very encouraging. That outlook—full of exhaustion, death, heartache, uncertainty, and unfairness—can lead to despair.
We need another view. Thankfully, **Genesis 2** gives us part of that. What we see here in this story reminds us of what is possible and the kind of life God longs to provide for us. As we study more, we will get an even fuller picture of what abundant life can look like even after sin came into the picture.

Small Group Discussion or Personal Reflection:
Thinking about the five Ps, where do you see these (or the lack of them) in your life?

What helps you personally flourish, abide, and stay connected to the Vine? What is one small practical thing you can do this week that may help you abide in His love?

Share prayer requests (if in a group) and close in prayer. If you're studying on your own, text or call a friend to see how you can pray for them this week and invite them to pray for you!

week 2
Digging Deeper

read
Read today's reading from the Bible:
Day 1 - Colossians 1:15-20
Day 2 - Psalm 8
Day 3 - Genesis 3
Day 4 - John 15:1-17
Day 5 - Romans 8:12-17

write
Pick one or two verses from today's reading and write the verse(s) out on the reflection pages provided or in your journal.

reflect
Use one or all of the following questions to reflect on the verses you read today:
1. Why did I pick the verse I did to write out? Are there any specific words or phrases that stood out to me?
2. What does today's reading tell me about God/Jesus?
3. What does today's reading tell me about abundant life?
4. What does this reading lead me to pray or do today?

prayer requests for this week:

week 2 notes & reflections

week 3
Life Shattered

Whether studying as a group or individually, recap the last few weeks of this study. Think or talk back through what you have studied so far.

Now, **read Genesis 3:1-7.**

Something I've learned throughout my life is that Satan's tricks don't really change. The methods may change but he always attacks life by stealing, killing, and destroying. One way he does this is by asking us the same question Eve heard in the garden: "Did God really say...?"

Did God really say He loves you?
Did God really say He wants to use you after all you've done?
Did God really say to take that leap of faith?

Where does Satan whisper "Did God really say...?" in your life?

Read Genesis 3:8-11.
Just like Satan's message hasn't really changed, neither has God's.
What are the first two questions God asks after Adam and Eve have fallen into sin?
-
-

What tone do you imagine God using as He said these things?

We cannot know for sure, but I think these are questions of pursuit and a broken heart. "*Where are you?*" shows us that He is a God who comes after us, even when—especially when—we mess up. The *"Who told you?"* question calls us to remember Whose voice matters most. It is almost as if He's saying, "I'm the One who gets to tell you who you are. I'm your Creator. No one else's opinions or thoughts matter more than mine. Listen to *Me*."

29

Which people or situations in your life tell you lies that lead to shame or sin?

Read Genesis 3:12-24.
Life as they knew it was changed. Think back to the Ps from last week:
The *perfection* is now shattered.
The *provision* and *protection* were still present but looked a little different and had extra boundaries.
Their *purpose* had shifted, and work became harder.
There was distance now instead of intimate nearness in their *personal relationship* with God.

Thinking back to Week 1 where we talked about John 10:10, we clearly see the impacts of Satan stealing, killing, and destroying and the impact of the fall into sin. It truly does lead to death—a "life" simply existing, surviving each day, and just barely getting through. We feel the impact of that day in the garden every day in our lives. And we hear those two questions of God: Where are you? Who told you?

In that place of tension, stuck between the garden of Eden and the garden of Eternity, maybe we find ourselves asking the same kind of questions a guy named Ezekiel asked when he was alive.

Ezekiel was a priest living in Jerusalem when the Babylonians attacked the city in 597 BC. They took the Israelites, including Ezekiel, into captivity in Babylon. In addition to being a priest, God also called him to serve as a prophet. In the first parts of the book, up through about chapter 35, we often see him called to prophesy *against* things, cities, or people. But as we get close to the section we're going to look at, it suddenly shifts and he's prophesying *to* things. Once a prophet telling of destruction, in the final chapters he gets to be a prophet of hope for the restoration God would bring after captivity.

Read Ezekiel 37:1-3.
What situations or areas of your life feel so dead they might as well be dry bones? Maybe it's a situation you wrote down at the end of the first week of study. Maybe you're thinking of someone so far from God you doubt they'll ever believe in Jesus. Maybe your daily routine feels monotonous and meaningless. Where are the dry and dead places? Where have you seen the perfection of life in Eden shattered?

God has a powerful message for Ezekiel amid a situation where the people of Israel were living lives as dry and dead as a valley of bones.

Read Ezekiel 37:4-14.
What are your thoughts and reactions to these verses?

As you look back at verse 5, we see almost a re-enactment of what we read last week. God breathes life into His people that they may live. In the story, God asked Ezekiel, *"Can these bones live?"* Ezekiel doesn't answer and God doesn't either. Instead, God shares this powerful message: **SPEAK LIFE!**

In the dead and dry situations of our lives, we may find ourselves saying along with Ezekiel, *"Oh, Lord, only You know if life is possible here."* The call of God to Ezekiel is the call for us today: SPEAK LIFE!

Our words matter. This isn't some kind of "name-it-claim-it" prosperity gospel situation where we just speak something into existence (only God has that power!). However, think about it in reverse for a minute. We all know gossip has power. Speaking negatively about someone shifts relationships, interactions, people's opinions, and ultimately that person's life *even if* the person isn't present when the words are spoken. Speaking life works the same way, but for the positive. Martin Luther's explanation of the eighth commandment also points to this reality:

> *"You shall not give false testimony against your neighbor. What does this mean? We should fear and love God so that we do not tell lies about our neighbor, betray him, slander him, or hurt his reputation,* **but defend him, speak well of him, and explain everything in the kindest way***" (emphasis added).* [1]

I once heard someone paraphrase **Ephesians 4:29** saying,
> *"Speak only words that make souls stronger."*

And **Proverbs 12:21** reminds us,
> *"The tongue has the power of life and death" (NIV).*

(Side note: this goes for how we speak about ourselves as well! Are you speaking life over yourself?!?)

We already looked back to how this event in Ezekiel re-enacts the Genesis 2 story we read last week where God gives humans life by breathing into them. If we look ahead to the New Testament, we also see this theme continue to weave through scripture.
Read Matthew 27:50-53 and John 20:22.

The word for *breath* and *spirit* in much of the Bible is the same original word. That is the case in these verses from Matthew. Jesus gave up his spirit/breath, and has He breathed out, people came back to life. It makes me think of the hymn "How Deep the Father's Love for Us" when it says: *"His dying breath has brought me life."* [2]

In the John passage we see life come through the Holy Spirit. We could do an entire study all about the breath of God, but for now we know it is a method by which He brings life. We navigate this earthly life in a way that goes beyond just survival, through dependance on the Holy Spirit inside us as believers! He is the one who restores and speaks life!

Small Group Discussion or Personal Reflection:
For good or harm, how have you experienced the reality that words matter and have power?

What could it look like practically to speak life this week over the dry and dead places around you?

Take a moment to revisit the "Praying For Life" section from week 1. Is there anything you want to add or update to your prayers there?

Close in prayer in your groups.

week 3
Digging Deeper

read
Read today's reading from the Bible:
Day 1 - Isaiah 61
Day 2 - Psalm 51
Day 3 - John 11:1-27
Day 4 - John 11:28-44
Day 5 - Romans 8:18-30

write
Pick one or two verses from today's reading and write the verse(s) out on the reflection pages provided or in your journal.

reflect
Use one or all of the following questions to reflect on the verses you read today:
1. Why did I pick the verse I did to write out? Are there any specific words or phrases that stood out to me?
2. What does today's reading tell me about God/Jesus?
3. What does today's reading tell me about abundant life?
4. What does this reading lead me to pray or do today?

prayer requests for this week:

week 3 notes & reflections

week 4

A Resurrected Life

Last week we talked about how sin shattered the perfect life God created back in Eden. We thought about the dead and dry places in our lives. Near the end of the study, we started to explore the ways God breathes life back into our souls. Today, we get a chance to study that theme more as we explore resurrection.

Often, we look for fixes to our problems and struggles. We long for things to be "just a little better." I once heard someone say something like, *"Jesus didn't come to make bad people good. He came to make dead people alive."*

In today's story we see a little of that tension. Lazarus is sick. His sisters, Mary and Martha, want healing for their brother (who also happens to be one of Jesus' best friends here on earth.)

Understandably, they want Jesus to come quickly and fix the situation, stopping the bad thing in their life from happening. Sometimes, this is exactly what God does.
Sometimes, though, death comes.

Read John 11:1-21.
I love the authenticity of Martha. Her relationship with Jesus is secure enough to "go there" and let Jesus walk her into life. Lazarus was not the only one facing a death of sorts. Mary and Martha had to face hard questions that day that could have resulted in the death of their faith. I can't help but wonder if they wrestled with questions like, *"Jesus, we've seen you heal strangers all over the place, but you let your friend die?!? What do we do with that?"*

Where have you seen sin cause chaos, destruction, or suffering and wondered why God didn't act or show up sooner?

Let's keep reading: John 11:22-32.
What do you notice about Martha and Mary's responses?

What I find fascinating is that they didn't run away from Jesus. They ran toward him. Martha came right away, and Mary followed as soon as she heard Jesus wanted to talk to her. They didn't avoid the hard, awkward questions; they engaged in the conversation.
What other thoughts, reactions, or questions come to mind as you hear this story?

Not only did Jesus raise Lazarus, but this was also a preview of His own death and resurrection.

Read Matthew 27:45-54.

We see so clearly here that in Jesus giving up His life, He brought life to others. But that's STILL not the end. This story may be familiar but try to read it as if hearing it for the first time and through the lens of God being a God of life.

Read Matthew 28:1-10.
What do you learn about God in this?

In verse 8 we see the women were *"frightened but also filled with great joy."* Our daily life involves being able to hold "both/ands." Fear AND joy. Sadness AND celebration. Often our lives in this earthly body have more than one emotion. There is tension, but a day is coming when all sorrow and sadness will end forever.
Read Revelation 21:1-5.

That day is coming. So, we must hold this tension. In the story of Lazarus' death, Jesus knew the end of the story for Lazarus and yet, He still wept. We hold the hope of a guaranteed perfect end to our story, while also living in the reality of a broken world. Not only is God in the business of bringing resurrection after death, but He also talks about other ways in His Word that He brings life OUT OF death.
Read John 12:20-36 and Romans 6:4.

What do you notice in these passages about the concept of life coming out of death?

Sometimes what feels like a "death" is really a "planting" with the goal of producing even more life. I'm struck by such similar language in these two passages. Death. Burial. New Lives.

What examples do you have of life coming through, after, or out of death?

In John 12:25 we hear the phrase "life in this world." This calls us to contrast "life in this world" to "eternal life." When we are willing to give up some of our focus on this earthly life, hope for the next life sneaks in and sustains us.

John 5:24, 17:3 and 1 John 5:11 remind us that eternal life has already begun. Those of us whom God has claimed as His children already *have* eternal life, in the present tense.

Small Group Discussion or Personal Reflection:
What is your normal reaction when someone disappoints you or you are confused by their actions? *(Do you engage? Push away? Ignore? Accuse? Jump to conclusions? Tell everyone except the person?)*

What does that look like in your relationship with God? Is it similar or different to how you interact with people?

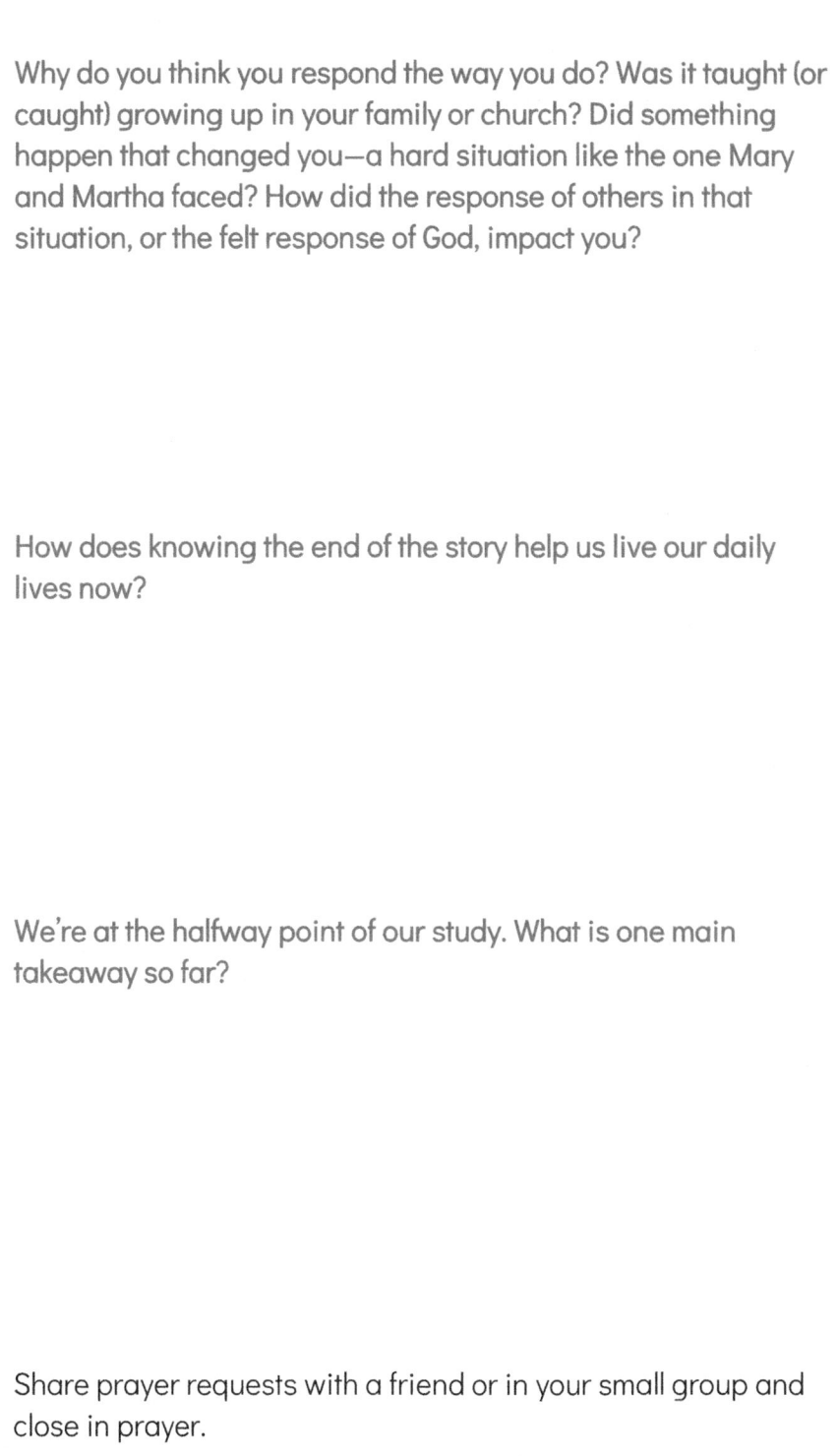

Why do you think you respond the way you do? Was it taught (or caught) growing up in your family or church? Did something happen that changed you—a hard situation like the one Mary and Martha faced? How did the response of others in that situation, or the felt response of God, impact you?

How does knowing the end of the story help us live our daily lives now?

We're at the halfway point of our study. What is one main takeaway so far?

Share prayer requests with a friend or in your small group and close in prayer.

week 4
Digging Deeper

read
Read today's reading from the Bible:
Day 1 - 1 Corinthians 15:12-22
Day 2 - Psalm 27
Day 3 - 1 John 5:11-21
Day 4 - John 12:20-36
Day 5 - Romans 8:31-39

write
Pick one or two verses from today's reading and write the verse(s) out on the reflection pages provided or in your journal.

reflect
Use one or all of the following questions to reflect on the verses you read today:
1. Why did I pick the verse I did to write out? Are there any specific words or phrases that stood out to me?
2. What does today's reading tell me about God/Jesus?
3. What does today's reading tell me about abundant life?
4. What does this reading lead me to pray or do today?

prayer requests for this week:

week 4 notes & reflections

week 5
Living with Hope

<u>Let's recap where we've journeyed so far:</u>
Week 1 - A God of Life
Week 2 - Life Begins
Week 3 - Life Shattered
Week 4 - A Resurrected Life

(If you are studying this with a group, consider talking briefly through each of the weeks and what you remember from each one. This is helpful to recall where we've been and is especially helpful for anyone who might have missed a week.)

So far, we have set the stage for how the concept of life is so important to God. We've seen the arc of it throughout the Bible. For the next few weeks, we're going to dig in a little deeper to characteristics of an abundant life.

Today, we're going to talk about *hope*.

Hope can be a kind of confusing concept. Sometimes, we hear the word, and we can breathe a little deeper. Remembering "there is hope here" brings peace. In other seasons, the concept of hope feels heartbreaking, especially when we don't see the things we hope for come to fruition or our hopes and dreams are shattered.

When you think of the word *hope* today, what comes to mind?

We're going to use the story of Sarai and Abram (later known as Sarah and Abraham) as we think about hope and promises. Their story shows us how living an abundant life means living with hope, even when it is difficult.

Let's head to Genesis and work our way through the story. It takes up multiple chapters, so we'll have to skim through it, but feel free to go back and read it all on your own as you have time.

- **Genesis 12** - Abram is seventy-five years old when he is called by God. The promise in Gen. 12:2 & 7 implies he would have children.
- **Genesis 13** – The promise is reiterated in verse 16.
- **Genesis 15** - The promise is clarified and sealed with a covenant.
- **Genesis 16** - Abram is eighty-six years old. He and Sarai wonder if perhaps they misunderstood the promise and took it into their own hands and he had a child with Sarai's servant instead of his wife.
- **Genesis 17** – Abram's name changed to Abraham and Sarai to Sarah. Abram is ninety-nine years old. God also promises that Sarah will be a mother of many nations, even at ninety years old. A timeline is given: "about this time next year" (verse 21).
- **Genesis 18** – The promise is reaffirmed where Sarah could hear.
- **Genesis 21** – *"The Lord kept His word and did for Sarah exactly what He had promised. She became pregnant and gave birth to a son..."* (21:1-2). Abraham is one hundred years old.

What do you notice about living with hope and following God from Abraham and Sarah's story?

This story covers multiple decades of life for this man and woman. That is a lot of waiting, a lot of hoping.

> ***Proverbs 13:12*** *says, "Hope deferred makes the heart sick, but a dream fulfilled is a tree of life" (NLT).*

God Himself tells us here that delayed, distracted, or denied hopes are not good for our souls. **So, what do we do when we get weary of waiting, when sin creeps in, and we are tempted to do things** our own way? What do we do when the answer to our hopes is delayed, or we hear "no"? How do you normally respond?

Centuries later in the New Testament, Paul recalls Sarah and Abraham's story. **Read Romans 4:18-25.**

What did Paul say Abraham did when hoping was hard? He kept hoping. **Verse 18** says, *"Against all hope, Abraham in hope believed" (NIV).* The New Living Translation (NLT) says, *"Even when there was no reason for hope, Abraham kept hoping..."*

We can do the same when we don't see situations play out how we desire. We can pay attention to our hopes. We can bring them to Jesus. We realign our expectations, and we remember our hope is secure in Him.

Against hope...we hope.

I once heard a sermon by Pastor Kevin Queen, in which he talked about three types of hope:
- Casual hopes - *e.g., "I hope we have something good for dinner tonight." "I hope it doesn't rain."*
- Precious hopes - *e.g., "I hope my loved one is healed from their disease." "I hope this dream of a child/marriage/job opportunity actually happens."*
- Ultimate hope - *Jesus. Only Jesus is our ultimate hope.*

Where we run into problems with hope is when we have our hopes in the wrong category. When what we want for dinner becomes a precious hope, or when we treat our ultimate hope in Jesus casually, that is when hope leads to discouragement, despair, discontent, and even death.

Let's head back to Abraham and Sarah's story. Their hope for a child was truly a precious hope. As their son Isaac grows, it seems hope might shatter once again. Their story takes a turn that can be hard to wrap our minds around when God asks Abraham to sacrifice his son, the very one that had been promised for decades.
Read Genesis 22:1-18.

Look at verses 7-8 - What animal is mentioned?

Now look at verse 13 - What animal is mentioned?

In most translations (and in the original Hebrew) the first animal mentioned is a lamb; then it says God provides a ram. Sometimes in our hopes, God provides a *"ram"* as He did for Abraham. Sometimes, He comes through, and our precious hopes are kept safe. Sometimes, He doesn't. Sometimes we're in a situation and no "ram" appears. Our precious hopes shatter. But no matter what, we do not lose our ultimate hope because He already has provided *The Lamb.* We can depend on the truth that Jesus is *"the Lamb of God who takes away the sin of the world" (John 1:29).* No matter whether our casual or precious hopes are fulfilled in this life or not, our ultimate hope in Jesus is 100 percent secure, always. He is here. He is with us. He will never leave. Our salvation is secure, and we know the end of the story. Let's pick back up where we left off in Romans.

Read Romans 5:1-5.
"And this hope will not lead to disappointment (put us to shame) For we know how dearly God loves us..." (verse 5, NLT; ESV).

Also consider **Psalm 25:3**
"No one who hopes in you will ever be put to shame."

While hoping for the fulfillment of our precious or casual hopes does occasionally come with risk of disappointment, our ultimate hope in

Jesus *never* does. In a life with Jesus, the word *hope* is not simply wishful thinking. It is a deep-rooted expectation of what is guaranteed to come. Abundant life flourishes when we understand that no matter what failures or disappointments come in this life, we are secure in the hands of a loving God who died for us. He is coming again. There will be a day when all our deepest hope will be fulfilled perfectly in His presence.

Small Group Discussion or Personal Reflection:
What are some of your casual or precious hopes right now?

What does it practically look like to hold those hopes, pray expectantly, trust God for those hopes, AND, at the same time, keep your *ultimate* hope in Jesus?

How does keeping our hopes in the right categories and our ultimate hope in Jesus lead to abundant life?

Spend time in prayer together or individually talking to God about your current hopes, dreams, prayers, or disappointments.

week 5
Digging Deeper

read
Read today's reading from the Bible:
Day 1 - 1 Peter 1:3-13
Day 2 - Psalm 25
Day 3 - John 4:1-26
Day 4 - John 4:27-42
Day 5 - Romans 5:1-11

write
Pick one or two verses from today's reading and write the verse(s) out on the reflection pages provided or in your journal

reflect
Use one or all of the following questions to reflect on the verses you read today:
1. Why did I pick the verse I did to write out? Are there any specific words or phrases that stood out to me?
2. What does today's reading tell me about God/Jesus?
3. What does today's reading tell me about abundant life?
4. What does this reading lead me to pray or do today?

prayer requests for this week:

week 5 notes & reflections

week 6

A Life of Purpose

Today we get to explore the concept of living water. Jesus talks about this in John 4 where we meet a nameless Samaritan woman. Before we dig into her story let's explore a little of the context.

Start by skimming through **John chapters 1-3**. **What has Jesus been up to so far in John's Gospel?**

Also, here is some context and information about the culture in that time and place that may be helpful before getting into the story:

- John 4:8 tells us that Jews did not talk to Samaritans. This is because of deep-rooted historical and religious tensions between these groups of people. When the Assyrians conquered the northern kingdom of Israel and later the Babylonians conquered the southern kingdom of Judah, both groups left behind some of the lowest classes of people. These people intermarried with non-Jewish people who slowly came into the region, and the Samaritans began as an ethnic and religious group. As horrible as it sounds, because of all this, the Jews considered the Samaritans "half-breeds."

- The Jews were also upset that the Samaritans built their own temple on Mount Gerizim, not in Jerusalem.

- In verse 4 we read that Jesus "had" to pass through Samaria. While it was the most direct route, because of the tensions described above, Jews almost always took a longer route around Samaria to get between Jerusalem and Galilee. His decision to go through instead of around Samaria was counter-cultural, yet intentional.

With all that in mind, let's read this story in **John 4:3-15.**

What do you notice about the way Jesus interacts with the woman in the story so far? What does He say? How does He engage the conversation?

What do you notice about how the woman responds to Jesus?

As we said before, Jews did not talk to Samaritans. Also, rabbis or teachers did not talk to women in public, often not even their wives or sisters. Women were deemed unable to understand "complicated topics" like theology and religion. Therefore, a Jewish male rabbi would *never* talk to a Samaritan woman. Yet, Jesus does.

Why do you think He goes against these cultural norms?

We also clearly see Jesus' humanity in this moment. He's tired. He's thirsty. When it comes to His interactions with the woman, one commentator states He also "is not unaware that the way to gain a soul is often to ask a service of it."[3] He asks her to meet a very practical need while offering to meet her deep spiritual need.

What do you think the Samaritan woman thought "living water" meant? How would you describe it?

Read John 4:16-42.
What do you notice now about Jesus' interaction with the woman and her response?

Here are a few things I noticed about this interaction:

Jesus sought her out.
Jesus *had* to go through Samaria. As we said before, this was not just for geographical reasons. I believe He felt He *had* to go there for that one woman. This echoes a little of the "where are you?" heart of God we talked about in Week 3.
Jesus is not here in flesh in the same way He was back then to show up at our kitchen sink. What does it look like or feel like now for Jesus to seek us out?

Jesus offers true life but doesn't force it upon people (verse 10).
In his commentary, David Guzik supports this point, saying, *"Jesus drew the woman into conversation, making her curious about many things. He made her curious about the things of God ("If you knew the gift of God"). He made her curious about who Jesus is ("who it is who says to you"). He made her curious about what He could give her ("He would have given you living water")."* [4]

Where have you seen it to be true that God offers abundant life but doesn't force it upon us?

61

Jesus got to the heart of the issue.

People did not typically go to the well in the hottest part of the day and women never did this alone...*unless* they were either trying to isolate themselves or had been cast out. Jesus sees this woman and engages with the hardest parts of her story. He wants to redeem her brokenness and restore her to the community.

If Jesus were sitting with you today at a coffee shop or other modern-day "well," what do you think He'd want to talk about? What would *you* want to talk about? How do you think He'd respond to you? (Carve out some time this week to sit and have this conversation with Jesus. Go for a walk. Sit and journal. Find a way to have that conversation.)

Jesus knew her and loved her anyway.

To be fully known and fully loved is perhaps our deepest desire. It can be scary to be known, but when it comes with unconditional love, it is beyond beautiful.

Tim Keller talks about this, saying,

"To be loved but not known is comforting but superficial. To be known and not loved is our greatest fear. But to be fully known and truly loved is, well, a lot like being loved by God. It is what we need more than anything. It liberates us from pretense, humbles us out of our self-righteousness, and fortifies us for any difficulty life can throw at us." [5]

If you have time this week, watch the YouTube video called "Woman at the Well" by lalaland481. In it the woman unpacks this story alongside the concept of being known and loved.

<u>Lastly, Jesus used her to help others know Him more.</u>
While some tell this story and assume the woman must have been promiscuous because of her five husbands, the reality is that a woman had no right to initiate a divorce in that culture. Even if she had been promiscuous (as she was living with a man who was not her husband), she had also either been discarded or widowed five times. The shame would have been intense. Despite her shame, despite her isolation, Jesus used her in powerful ways for the kingdom. The entire town came to know Jesus because of her.

This is the core of today's study:
Living water leads to a life of purpose.

Read 2 Timothy 1:9 & Ephesians 4:1.
These verses talk about our purpose and calling. Having a sense of meaning is a critical piece of abundant life.

Go back to **John 4:13-14.**

These verses tell us that when we are filled with living water, it naturally creates a fountain that brings life to others. In verses 39-41 we read that some of the people in her town believed in Jesus because of her testimony. Then, they got to know Jesus themselves. Not only did God restore her life individually, but He also gave her a sense of renewed purpose as she engaged with those around her.

How do you see this to be true: an abundant life involves a life with purpose and meaning? (This could be in the sense that abundant life gives purpose, or that having purpose brings life.)

Last week in John 11, we heard Mary and Martha use the phrase "if only" when they cried out to Jesus, *"Lord, if only you had been here, [our] brother would not have died"* (verses 21, 32).
In today's story, the woman might have been thinking "if only" as well. *"If only you knew who I was, you wouldn't talk to me. If only you knew what I've done, you wouldn't ask me for anything."*

In this story, Jesus is actually the one saying, "if only." He says, *"If you only knew the gift God has for you..."* (John 4:10, NLT).

Jesus often does that, doesn't He? We have moments when we tell Him, "if only you had been here" or "if only you knew!" And with love in His heart and compassion in His eyes, He looks at us and longs for us to know what He knows. He longs for us to know the gift God has for us even if it may be hard to see at times.

Small Group Discussion or Personal Reflection:
Where does "if only" come into your conversations with God? What kinds of things make you wonder, "If only You had been here..." or "If only You knew..."?

How might Jesus fill in this phrase if He was speaking to you today about the ways He wants to bring purpose and abundant life to you? What do you think God desperately wants you to know right now?

_____, if you only knew_____
(Name)

_____.

(Can't think of one? Maybe try this: "If only you knew how much I love you!")

If you are studying in a group, consider sharing what you wrote in the blank as you wrap up your time together and close in prayer.

week 6
Digging Deeper

read
Read today's reading from the Bible:
Day 1 - 1 Peter 2:4-10
Day 2 - Psalm 90
Day 3 - 2 Timothy 1
Day 4 - John 21:15-19
Day 5 - Romans 5:12-21

write
Pick one or two verses from today's reading and write the verse(s) out on the reflection pages provided or in your journal.

reflect
Use one or all of the following questions to reflect on the verses you read today:
1. Why did I pick the verse I did to write out? Are there any specific words or phrases that stood out to me?
2. What does today's reading tell me about God/Jesus?
3. What does today's reading tell me about abundant life?
4. What does this reading lead me to pray or do today?

prayer requests for this week:

week 6 notes & reflections

week 7
Living in Freedom

I first wrote this study for a group of dear women at my church. A few weeks before the series began, I suddenly became a temporary guardian for a seventeen-year-old. As one might imagine, this was quite an adjustment to my life and schedule. So, instead of having the series finished before the study started as I planned, I often finished each week's outline during the week in which I was teaching it.

During week 7, some things happened both in our home and at work that left me with considerably less time to prepare and meant our study was a little less put-together than I like. As irony would have it, I had a chance to live out the very thing we will be talking about in this lesson: living in freedom.

"Abundant life" and "freedom" for me that week meant choosing not to worry about having everything perfect but just showing up anyway to connect with those other women and Jesus through His Word! While I did do a little editing before publishing this study, I chose to leave this session more open-ended, just like my friends and I experienced our first time through it. I trust that the Holy Spirit will show up for you today and show you what He wants you to see in His Word just like He did for us.

Skim through Exodus 12-16, perhaps looking at chapter headings. What are some of the main parts of the story you notice as you skim or remember if you have read it before?

This is the story of God rescuing his people from slavery in Egypt. Finally, they are free. Yet, they start grumbling and want to go back **(Exodus 14:11-12, 12:11-12, 15:22-16:3).**

Why do you think they had such a strong desire in that moment to return to slavery? Why might they have thought surviving in slavery was better than the abundant life God had waiting for them (eventually) in the Promised Land?

If we fast forward to the New Testament, a similar thing happened in a spiritual sense for some believers during the time after Jesus' life, death, and resurrection. We read about it in the letter called Galatians. The believers of Galatia eagerly trusted the beautiful gospel of God but then quickly returned to the slavery of sin and trying to earn their own salvation (**see Galatians 1:6-7**). The whole book of Galatians is a call to the freedom of God's grace. Let's dig in a little more and **read Galatians chapter 5**.

While they had at first believed that there was nothing they could do to earn their salvation, they were starting to question that. Some Jews were trying to convince them that it would take faith AND circumcision—faith AND some act on their own—to be saved. They quickly forgot that the grace and forgiveness of Jesus on the cross alone is more than enough.

In today's world, where do you hear "faith AND ____" messages? Where are we tempted to try to add qualifications on God's grace?

What does this chapter of Galatians tell us about freedom and it being a characteristic of abundant life?

How do you think abundant life relates to freedom? What other stories or situations come to mind either in scripture or life that connect these two concepts?

There are many ways to live in the freedom of Christ. One practice that comes to mind is God's call to Sabbath rest. Throughout scripture we are invited to practice a period of time each week to rest and remember God. This is even a command found in the Ten Commandments. We find these commandments in two places in scripture. What is fascinating to note, though, is that while almost everything about the two sections of scripture is identical, the rationale behind Sabbath is slightly different in Exodus than Deuteronomy.

Read Exodus 20:8-10.
Here, the reason for resting on the Sabbath was as a call to mimic God resting on the seventh day of Creation.

Now, read Deuteronomy 5:12-15.
When those commands were shared again here, the reason given was to remember their time in slavery and the call to freedom.

Mark Buchanan explains it this way in his book, *The Rest of God*:
"Exodus grounds Sabbath in creation. Deuteronomy grounds it in liberation. Exodus remembers Eden, Deuteronomy Egypt....Slaves don't rest. Slaves can't rest. Slaves, by definition, have no freedom to rest. Rest, it turns out, is a condition of liberty. God calls us to live in the freedom that he won for us with his own outstretched arm. Sabbath is a refusal to go back to Egypt." [6]

God longs to bring us freedom from the things that enslave us. He did this ultimately through His death on the cross and resurrection. Where we were once slave to sin, we now get to walk in the freedom and joy of abundant life.

Small Group Discussion or Personal Reflection:
Think of a time when you found yourself struggling to live in freedom or went back to the slavery of sin. What was your reason for doing so?

Sabbath is one practical way to practice freedom. What other ways could you practice living in the abundant, free life of Christ? What could that look like for you in this season?

What other thoughts or reflections do you have about freedom as a characteristic of living an abundant life?

Check back in on your "Praying for Life" page from week 1. Are there updates to share with the group or other prayer requests this week?

week 7
Digging Deeper

read
Read today's reading from the Bible:
Day 1 - Acts 2:42-47
Day 2 - Psalm 78:1-39
Day 3 - Psalm 78:40-72
Day 4 - John 8:31-36
Day 5 - Romans 6:1-14

write
Pick one or two verses from today's reading and write the verse(s) out on the reflection pages provided or in your journal.

reflect
Use one or all of the following questions to reflect on the verses you read today:
1. Why did I pick the verse I did to write out? Are there any specific words or phrases that stood out to me?
2. What does today's reading tell me about God/Jesus?
3. What does today's reading tell me about abundant life?
4. What does this reading lead me to pray or do today?

prayer requests for this week:

week 7 notes & reflections

week 8

Life Forever

Here we are, already at the end of our time together. Let's recap a little of our journey.

In week 1, we explored the idea that our God is a God of life! Life is something He is passionate about. We serve a living God who brings us life. Depending on the translation there are more than twenty names for God throughout scripture that use the words *life* or *living* in them. It really must matter to Him and be something He wants to be known for. This also set the stage for the whole study exploring what it means in John 10:10 for Jesus to bring us abundant life.

Over the next few weeks, we explored the beginning of human life, which was created beautiful and perfect. That perfection was shattered, but God has been on a mission ever since to bring restoration and resurrection. We journeyed with Adam and Eve, Ezekiel, Mary, Martha, and Lazarus as God showed up in each of their stories to bring life to the places that were dead.

The last weeks of the study we explored a few characteristics that are part of an abundant life: hope, purpose, and freedom.

Abraham and Sarah became our companions in week 5 as we learned why a life of abundance is a life of hope, even when (maybe especially when) situations seem hopeless.

Through Jesus' interactions with the Samaritan woman at the well and then her interactions with others in her city, we discovered that inviting others into the abundant life Jesus offers brings us purpose and meaning.

Finally, last week we talked about the things that keep us trapped in slavery instead of freedom. Along with the Israelites and the people of Galatia, God invites us to practice freedom as a way to truly live.

Thinking back on this whole study so far, what are one or two things that caught your attention or that you want to remember? If studying with a group, share these things with one or two people around you..

What things about abundant life still have you curious? What might you want to explore even more on your own in the future?

One last concept we want to explore together about abundant life is the idea that life in Christ never actually ends. Back on week 2 when we talked about the start of human life, we saw death was never in God's original design. Because of what Jesus has done on the cross and the fact that He will return, there is life beyond death.

To explore a little more of what that might mean for us today, let's explore Revelation 21 and 22. This final book of the Bible recounts the revelation given to John by an angel near the end of his earthly life. The first verse of the book tells us the purpose of this book is to show God's servants what is to come. Let's fast forward to the very end.

Read Revelation 21:1-7, 22-27.
What does this tell us about abundant life that is to come?

What does this tell us about God?

What does this tell us about us and our future?

One of my favorite things about this section is the reminder that restoration is coming. All the things that break our heart, all the things that are a result of abundant life being shattered back in Genesis 3, all the sorrow and tears and death itself, *WILL* be gone forever one day, never to return.

Let's continue reading a little further and see what else it tells us.

Read Revelation 22:1-6,14.

Does anything sound familiar from verse 2? The tree of life is back on the scene! In Genesis 3, humans were protected by being banned from access to this tree temporarily, until God could set things right. One day that access will be restored. We will once again be able to eat freely from the tree of life, *"and the leaves of the tree are for the healing of the nations" (verse 2).*

We discovered throughout the last seven weeks that God desires to give us abundant life. He doesn't force it on us. He is patient with us like He was with the Israelites wanting to go back to slavery. He carries us in seasons where it's hard to stay hopeful like He did with Abraham and Sarah. He even brings dead things back to life as He did with Lazarus and Ezekiel. He does all that with the long view in mind—the goal of restoring everything fully and completely.

"The Spirit and the Bride say, 'Come.' And let the one who hears say, 'Come.' And let the one who is thirsty come; let the one who desires take the water of life without price.....He who testifies to these things says, 'Surely I am coming soon.' Amen. Come, Lord Jesus!" (Revelation 22:17,20).

How does hope in our future reality change life here and now?

Back on the first day of this study you were invited to write down situations in which you were asking God to bring abundant life. Go back to that "Praying for Life" page or look at the very first question of the study on page 7 where you noted places you see Satan stealing, killing, or destroying.

Consider for yourself or share with someone how you have seen God bring life to those situations. You may be able to note dramatic resurrection like Lazarus or it may feel like the situation is still as dead and dry as the bones in Ezekiel's story. No matter which is truer, I trust that God has shown up in some way regarding that situation, even if it was simply adding clarity around how to pray. Note what you have seen below or share with a friend.

On day 1, we read these words from the very end of John's Gospel:
"Jesus performed many other signs in the presence of
his disciples, which are not recorded in this book.
But these are written that you may believe
that Jesus is the Messiah, the Son of God, and
that by believing you may have life in his name."
(John 20:30-31, emphasis added).

John wrote down the stories he saw and witnessed so that we might have life. God gives the chance to invite others into life as well. Revelation 22:17 (on page 83) says that not only does the Spirit invite the thirsty to come, but also the Bride, His Church, us. We hear the call to "come" and then we get to say "come" to others!

Who is God calling you to invite into abundant life?
What is He calling you to do in the near future as you interact with that person?

Now that we've spent seven weeks studying it, how would you describe abundant life? What does it look like, sound like, or feel like to truly live?

Father, Jesus, Spirit,
We praise you that You are a God of Life! Keep showing us how to live in your joy, freedom, hope, and love every single day. Lead us into the dry and parched places of this world as your Church to be a people who point to You, our Living Water. We look forward to the day when we get to experience perfect life with you, forever! Amen!

week 8
digging deeper

review & reflect
Skim back through the entire study and make a list of a few things you want to remember as we wrap up this time together.

looking ahead
Consider what's next for you as you wrap up this study. What rhythms of connecting with God though His Word, prayer, and community feel like they'd help you live abundantly in the days, weeks, and months ahead?

a sending blessing

"I pray that from his glorious, unlimited resources he will empower you with inner strength through his Spirit. Then Christ will make his home in your hearts as you trust in him. Your roots will grow down into God's love and keep you strong. And may you have the power to understand, as all God's people should, how wide, how long, how high, and how deep his love is. May you experience the love of Christ, though it is too great to understand fully. Then you will be made complete with all the fullness of life and power that comes from God. Now all glory to God, who is able, through his mighty power at work within us, to accomplish infinitely more than we might ask or think. Glory to him in the church and in Christ Jesus through all generations forever and ever! Amen."
Ephesians 3:16-21 (NLT)

final notes & reflections

thank you!

To My Family, Friends, & Teammates – I am grateful that the most common way God brings abundant life is through the people around us. Through you, God truly fills my life with joy, peace, and hope.

To the Wednesday Night Calvary Ladies – Thank you for taking this journey with me first. I didn't necessarily set out to publish a Bible Study. I just cherished the chance to explore what I was learning with you and as you bravely reflected, studied, and shared, this was born.

To the Vineyard Family – Jenny, you watered a little seed when you somewhat jokingly asked, "So, when are you publishing this?" Thanks to each of you for showing me every day what it means to truly live!

To Becky and the Chen Family – Thanks for always being some of my biggest cheerleaders in life! This project was no exception!

To Ryan and Sarah – Thank you for walking with me to find new life in this season and Ryan, thank you for following the Spirit's leading with that prayer in chapel months ago. This is just one of many ways I've seen God answer.

To Nicole – Thanks for being the first to journey through this on your own, making sure I wasn't lying on the front cover when I said it could work for groups AND individuals.

To My Students – As the dedication at the front of the book says, one of my biggest prayers is that you come to know not only the abundant life Jesus has for you, but also His abundant LOVE. I am grateful for the ways you teach me daily what it means to be fully alive!

To Jesus – You *are* my Life. I'm humbled, joyful, & grateful that we get to do this life together... *forever!*

Notes

[1] Martin Luther, "The Ten Commandments," Luther's Small Catechism, 2019, https://catechism.cph.org/en/10-commandments-eighth.html.
[2] Townsend, Stuart. "How Deep the Father's Love for Us." Thankyou Music, 1995.
[3] Godet, cited by David Guzik, "Enduring Word Bible Commentary John Chapter 4," Enduring Word, 2018, https://enduringword.com/bible-commentary/john-4/.
[4] David Guzik, "Enduring Word Bible Commentary John Chapter 4," Enduring Word, 2018, https://enduringword.com/bible-commentary/john-4/.
[5] Timothy Keller and Kathy Keller, *The Meaning of Marriage: Facing the Complexities of Commitment with the Wisdom of God* (New York, NY: Penguin Books, 2016).
[6] Mark Buchanan, *The Rest of God: Restoring Your Soul by Restoring Sabbath* (Nashville, TN: Thomas Nelson, 2007), 87-90.

Made in the USA
Coppell, TX
03 April 2024